A CALL TO PRAYER

IN TODAY'S ENGLISH WITH INTRODUCTION
AND A STUDY GUIDE

J. C. RYLE

GODLIPRESS TEAM

© Copyright 2023 by GodliPress. All rights reserved.

This book is copyright protected. You cannot amend, distribute, sell, use, quote or paraphrase any part, or the content within this book, without the consent of the author or publisher, except in the case of brief quotations embodied in critical articles or reviews.

Scripture quotations are from The ESV® Bible (The Holy Bible, English Standard Version®), copyright © 2001 by Crossway, a publishing ministry of Good News Publishers. Used by permission. All rights reserved.

CONTENTS

Introduction	v
1. THE QUESTION	1
2. PRAYER IS NECESSARY FOR SALVATION	3
Why Is It Necessary?	3
It's Your Responsibility	4
Study Guide	5
3. PRAYER AS A HABIT IS THE SIGN OF A TRUE CHRISTIAN	7
Christians that Pray	7
Christians that Don't Pray	9
Evidence of Prayer	9
Study Guide	11
4. PRAYER IS THE MOST NEGLECTED DUTY	12
Why People Don't Pray	14
Study Guide	16
5. PRAYER BRINGS ENCOURAGEMENT	18
God's Part in Prayer	18
His Promises	20
Study Guide	22
6. DILIGENT PRAYER IS THE SECRET TO HOLINESS	23
Two Different Types of Christian	23
What Is the Difference?	25
Study Guide	27
7. PRAYER AND BACKSLIDING	29
What Is Backsliding?	29
Why Christians Backslide	30
Study Guide	31

8. PRAYER AND CONTENTMENT — 33
   Prayer Is the Answer — 34
   Jesus Will Take Our Sorrows — 35
   Study Guide — 37

9. TO THOSE WHO DON'T PRAY — 38
   No Excuse for Not Praying — 38
   A Warning — 40
   Study Guide — 40

10. TO THOSE WHO WANT SALVATION — 42
    Taking the First Step — 42
    Don't Doubt — 44
    Study Guide — 45

11. TO THOSE WHO PRAY — 46
    Reverence and Humility in Prayer — 47
    Praying Spiritually — 48
    Regular Prayer — 49
    Perseverance in Prayer — 49
    Sincerity in Prayer — 50
    Praying with Faith — 52
    Boldness in Prayer — 53
    Fullness in Prayer — 54
    Specific Prayer — 55
    Intercession in Prayer — 56
    Gratitude in Prayer — 57
    Being Alert in Prayer — 58
    Study Guide — 59

Notes — 61
About J. C. Ryle — 63
Bibliography — 65
Notes — 67
Notes — 69
Notes — 71

INTRODUCTION

The topic of prayer has either been so saturated with books that it has become a diluted subject, or it has been passed over for more enticing spiritual topics and left to gather dust. For most of us Christians, we are often stuck in the middle somewhere and find ourselves like that person James describes in chapter 1:6 *"driven and tossed by the wind."* This seems to sum up the majority of our prayer lives—spurts of enthusiasm and long, dry stretches of silence.

J.C. Ryle tackles the issue of prayer head-on but in a very personal approach that speaks to each of our hearts. He leaves no one out and takes time to address those who pray, those who don't, and those who are yet to come to Jesus. He opens the door wide for every one of us to enter into what he calls "the mightiest weapon God has placed in our hands."

Originally written as a tract, a short exposition on prayer, this treasure has taken on book form and been published many times over. It has survived to become a classic since the late 1800s to this modern age and can often be found among other prominent volumes on bookshelves around the world. The message contained, though, has not changed, summed up in J.C. Ryle's repeated question: DO YOU PRAY?

As an overseer of churches and a minister, there is a distinct pastoral heart behind Ryle's words. Rather than accusing us of lacking in prayer or being guilty of neglect, he admits that we all suffer similar drawbacks when it comes to this key element of Christianity. He encourages, offers guidance, gives practical steps, and in this his desire to see all believers grow is evident.

Bringing this classic into today's English, we have been careful to capture the same heart and the same urgency that Ryle wrote over a hundred years ago. Added to that, the study guide allows a wonderful opportunity to delve deeper into the subject of prayer, as well as to reflect on our own hearts in this matter.

This book was written to challenge and encourage, and as J.C. Ryle said, "to make us think, to wean us from the world, to send us to the Bible, to drive us to our knees."

1
THE QUESTION

"They ought always to pray"
Luke 18:1

"I desire then that in every place the men should pray"
1 Tim 2:8

I ask you an extremely important question. It's the title that your eyes first see written in those three little words —Do you pray?

The question is one that only you can answer. Whether you go to church or not, your pastor knows. Whether you have family prayers in your house or not, your relatives will know.

But whether you pray in private or not, is a matter between yourself and God.

In love, I beg you to seriously consider what I am asking. Don't say that my question is too close for comfort. If your heart is right before God, there should be nothing to be afraid of. Don't try to sweep away my question by replying that you say your prayers. It's one thing to say your prayers, and another to pray. Don't tell me that my question is unnecessary. Take a few minutes, and I will show you good reasons for asking it.

2
PRAYER IS NECESSARY FOR SALVATION

Why Is It Necessary?

I deliberately use the words 'absolutely necessary.' I am not speaking now about babies and those who cannot think for themselves. I am not talking about the lost who are not yet saved. I know that where little is given, little will be required. I speak specifically to anyone who calls themselves a Christian. Those men and women who do not pray, cannot be born again.

I believe in salvation by grace as much as anyone else. I would gladly offer free and full forgiveness to the greatest sinner that ever lived, and stand by his death bed, and say, *"Believe in the Lord Jesus, and you will be saved"* (Acts 16:31). But I cannot see in the Bible that someone can have salvation without asking for it. For someone to receive forgiveness of his sins, but not lift up their heart, and say, "Lord Jesus, give it to me," I cannot find this anywhere. I can find evidence that no one can be saved by their prayers, but I can't find any that says you will be saved without prayer.

It is not absolutely necessary for salvation that you have to read the Bible. You might have no education, or be blind, and yet have Jesus in your heart. It is not absolutely necessary that you must publicly hear the preaching of the Gospel. He might live where the Gospel is not preached, or be confined to your bed, or deaf. But the same cannot be said about prayer. It is absolutely necessary for salvation that you pray.

It's Your Responsibility

There is no easy, quick, royal path to health or learning. Princes and kings, poor men and workers, all have to attend to the needs of their own bodies and minds. No one can eat, drink, or sleep by proxy or through someone else. No one can have another person learn the alphabet for them. All these are things everybody must do for himself, or they will never be done.

Just as it is with the mind and body, so it is with the heart. There are certain things absolutely necessary for the heart's health and well-being. Each person has to look after these things for themselves. Each must repent for themselves. Each must come to Jesus for themselves. And each person must speak to God and pray. You must do it for yourself because nobody else can do it for you.

How can you expect to be saved by an 'unknown' God? And how can you know God without prayer? You know nothing of men and women in this world unless you speak to them. You cannot know Jesus as God unless you speak to Him in prayer. If you want to be with Him in heaven one day, you must be one of His friends on earth now. If you want to be one of His friends on earth, you must pray.

There will be many people at Jesus' right hand on the last day. All the saints gathered from north and south, and east and west will be a crowd that no one will be able to count. The song of victory that will come from their mouths, when their redemption is finally complete, will be a glorious song. It will be more than the noise of many rivers and mighty thunders, but there will be no one out of tune in that song, only harmony. They will sing with one heart and one voice; their experiences will be the same. All of them will have believed. All of them will have been washed in the blood of Jesus. All of them will have been born again. All of them will have prayed. Yes, we must pray on earth, or we will never praise in heaven.

We must go through the school of prayer, or we will never be ready for the time of praise.

To be prayerless is to be without God—without Jesus, without grace, without hope, and without heaven. It is as good as being on the road to hell. Now, can you understand why I ask the question—DO YOU PRAY?

Study Guide

We often take it for granted that our salvation requires an exchange with Jesus—a confession, response, acknowledgment of who God is. This is prayer. As Ryle points out, it is not simply an extra benefit or something to be attained later as a mature Christian but is the first act of accepting Jesus into our hearts. It is a vital aspect of becoming and being a Christian.

Treat this study guide as a guide—it is simply a tool for you to think more on certain questions that are raised in the book concerning your own life. Use them in your group Bible study or on your own as you see fit.

1. What do you think of the statement that nobody "can have salvation without asking for it"?
2. Look at Romans 10:13, Joel 2:32, and Romans 10:9 and discuss these verses in this regard.
3. The same way we look after the body and mind, we should take care or exercise the heart. What are the ways we do this?
4. "To be prayerless is to be without God—without Jesus, without grace, without hope, and without heaven." What do you make of this strong statement?
5. Can you remember your salvation? Was some kind of prayer involved?

3

PRAYER AS A HABIT IS THE SIGN OF A TRUE CHRISTIAN

Christians that Pray

All Christians are the same in this respect. From the moment there is any life and reality about their beliefs and faith, they pray. Just as the first sign of life in a baby when it's born is the act of breathing, so the first act of men and women when they are born again is praying.

This is one of the common signs of those chosen by God, "*Who cry to him day and night*" (Luke 18:7). The Holy Spirit, who makes us new creatures, gives us the feeling of adoption and makes us cry, "*Abba, Father*" (Rom 8:15). Jesus, when He gives us new life, also gives us a voice and a tongue, and says to us, "*Be no longer mute*" (Ezek 24:27). God has no mute children that can't speak. Praying is as much a part of our new nature as it is for a baby to cry. We see our need for mercy and grace. We feel our emptiness and weakness. We can't do anything differently than what they do. We must pray.

I have looked carefully over the lives of God's people in the Bible. I can't find one whose history is told to us, from Genesis to Revelation, who was not a man of prayer. It is mentioned as a characteristic of those who are godly; that *"call on him as Father"* that *"call upon the name of our Lord Jesus Christ"* The characteristic of the wicked is recorded as those who *"do not call upon the Lord"* (1 Peter 1:17; 1 Cor 1:2; Psalm 14:4).

I have read about the lives of many prominent Christians who have lived since the Bible days. Some of them were rich and some poor. Some were educated, and some were not. Some of them were Episcopalians, some Presbyterians, some Baptists, some Independents, some Wesleyans. Some were Calvinists and some Arminians. Some loved to use liturgy and prayer books, and some used nothing. But one thing that they all had in common: They were all men of prayer.

Looking at the reports of missionaries, we are glad when we see men and women are receiving the Gospel all over the world. There are conversions in Africa, in New Zealand, in Asia, in America. Those who are born again are obviously different from each other in culture, nationality, and language. But there is one striking similarity we can observe: People who are born again always pray.

Christians that Don't Pray

I don't deny that some might pray without engaging their heart and without sincerity. I don't pretend to say that just because a person is praying proves everything about their heart. As in every other part of religion, there is plenty of deception and hypocrisy.

But I will say this—not praying is clear proof that a person is not a true Christian. He can't really feel his sins. He can't love God. He can't feel indebted to Christ. He can't long for holiness. He can't desire heaven. He must still be born again. He must still be made a new creature. He might confidently boast of being chosen by God, having grace, faith, hope, and knowledge, and might be able to deceive ignorant people. But it all means nothing if he doesn't pray.

Evidence of Prayer

And I also add that of all the evidence of a real work of the Spirit, the habit of sincere, private prayer is one of the most acceptable ones. A man can preach from false motives. He can write books, make fine speeches, and seem diligent in good works, but still be a Judas Iscariot. But someone hardly ever goes into his room and pours out his soul before God in secret unless they are sincere. God has put His stamp on prayer as the best proof of true conversion. When He sent Ananias to Saul in Damascus, He gave him no other evidence of his change of heart than this—"*Behold, he is praying*" (Acts 9:11).

I know that much can go on in a person's mind before they come to pray. They might have many convictions, desires, wishes, feelings, intentions, resolutions, hopes, and fears. But all these things are not very clear evidence. They can all be found in ungodly people as well and often end in nothing. In many cases, they don't last longer than the morning mist or the dew that passes away. A real, sincere prayer, flowing from a broken and contrite spirit, is worth more than all these things put together.

I know that Christians are called to salvation for all eternity. I know that the Holy Spirit, who calls us at the right time, often leads us by very slow degrees in our relationship with Jesus. But our human eyes can only judge by what they see. I can't call anyone justified until he believes. I will not say that any one believes until he prays. I can't understand a mute faith; the first act of faith is to speak to God. Faith is to the heart what life is to the body. Prayer is to faith what breath is to life. How someone can live and not breathe is beyond comprehension, and how someone can believe and not pray is beyond comprehension too.

Don't be surprised if you hear preachers spending a lot of time on the importance of prayer. This is the point we want to bring you to—we want to know that you are praying. Your doctrinal views may be correct, and your love of the true Gospel may be unmistakable, but this could be nothing more than head knowledge and outward works. We want to know whether you actually know the throne of grace and whether you can speak to God as well as speak about God.

Do you wish to find out if you are a true Christian or not? Then you will see that my question is very important—DO YOU PRAY?

Study Guide

This chapter makes a strong argument for what a true Christian is or isn't, purely by the presence or lack of prayer in their lives. Often, our criteria stops at the moment a person is converted or born again. But here, it talks about people who pray—as a lifestyle!

These questions are good to understand the chapter better, but they can also be used in reflecting on your own prayer life. This might make you feel exposed or reveal areas that you would rather not acknowledge, but this is the best way to bring them to the Lord and ask Him to help you to change.

1. It says that Jesus gives a tongue and voice to pray. Do you think, as unbelievers, we had these, or did we receive them once being born again?
2. Psalm 14:4 is very clear. What do you understand by it?
3. Ryle lists a few proofs that a person who doesn't pray cannot be a Christian. What are they?
4. Can you describe what real, sincere prayer is?
5. How would you rate your prayer life on a scale of 1-10 (1 being non-existent to 10 as perfect)?

4
PRAYER IS THE MOST NEGLECTED DUTY

We live in a time when there are so many people in the religious profession. There are more churches now than there ever were before, and many people are attending them. And yet, despite all this public religion, I believe there is huge neglect of personal prayer.

A few years ago, I would not have said that. In my ignorance, I thought that most Christians said their prayers, and many people prayed. But now, I see it differently, and I have concluded that the most professing Christians do not pray at all.

Prayer Is Ignored and Rushed

I know this sounds very shocking and will surprise many, but I am convinced that prayer is just something which is thought to be a 'matter of course,' and like many matters of course is badly neglected. It is 'everybody's business,' and so, is a business carried out by very few people. It's one of those private transactions between God and our souls that no one can see, and therefore has the temptation to pass over and leave it undone.

I believe that thousands of people never say a word of prayer at all. They eat, drink, sleep, rise, go to work, and return to their homes. They breathe God's air, see His sun, walk on His earth, and enjoy His mercies. They have bodies that will die and have judgment and eternity before them, but they never speak to God. They live like the animals that die, behave like creatures without souls, and have nothing to say to Him who holds their life, breath, and all things, and from whose mouth they will one day receive their everlasting sentence. It is terrible, but also, unfortunately, very common!

I believe there are tens of thousands whose prayers are just a set of words repeated by rote, without a thought about their meaning. Some say a few quick sentences they picked up in the school when they were children. Some are content with repeating the words, forgetting that there is no real request in it. Some add the Lord's Prayer, but without the slightest desire that the serious things they ask for will be granted. Some who are homeless, simply repeat the old lines: "Matthew, Mark, Luke, and John, bless the bed that I lie on."

Many, even those people who use the correct style and manner, mutter their prayers quickly after they have got into bed, or scramble over them while they wash or dress in the morning. They can think what they want, but in the sight of

God, this is not praying. Words said without heart are as useless to our souls as the drum-beating of heathens before their idols. Where there is no heart, there may be lip service, but there is nothing that God listens to—there is no prayer. Saul, I have no doubt, said many long prayers before the Lord met him on the way to Damascus. But it was not until his heart was broken that God said, "*he is praying*" (Acts 9:11).

Does this surprise you? Let me show you that I am not speaking nonsense. Do you think that my statements are over-the-top and without substance? Give me your attention, and I will show you that I am only telling you the truth.

Why People Don't Pray

Have you forgotten that it is not natural for anyone to pray? The carnal, human mind is in opposition to God. Man's heart desires to get far away from God and have nothing to do with Him. His feeling toward Him is not love but fear. Why should a man pray when he has no real sense of sin, no real feeling of spiritual need, no belief in unseen things, no desire for holiness and heaven? Most men know and feel nothing about any of these things; they are walking in the broad way. It's very clear to me, so I will say it boldly: I believe that few people pray.

Do you not know that it's unfashionable to pray? It's just one of the things that many are ashamed to admit to doing. Hundreds would much rather head to a cliff edge or follow a lost hope than publicly confess that they pray every day. If forced to sleep in the same room as a stranger, many would go to bed without prayer than speaking to God in front of the other person. To drive well, to dress well, to go out, to be thought of as clever and agreeable—all this is fashionable, but not to pray. I can't state it clearly enough. It's unbelievable that so many people are ashamed of a habit that is supposed to be common. I believe that few people pray.

Have you thought about the lives that many live? Is it realistic to imagine that people are praying against sin every day and night when we see them embracing sin? Is it possible that they pray against the world when they are entirely absorbed and caught up in its pursuits? Do we really think they ask God for grace to serve Him when they don't show the slightest desire to serve Him at all? No! It's very obvious and clear that most people either ask nothing from God or don't mean what they say when they do ask—which is the same thing. Praying and sinning will never live together in the same heart. Prayer will consume sin, or sin will choke prayer. I can't let this go when I look at men's lives. I believe that few people pray.

Are you not aware of how many people are dying? When they are close to death, they are like strangers to God. Not only are they ignorant of His Gospel, but they have no power to speak to Him. Their efforts to reach God in those moments are painfully awkward, shy, and raw as if they are doing it for the first time. It's as if they need an introduction to God, and as if they had never talked with Him before. I remember hearing about a lady who was worried to have a pastor come and visit her when she was sick and dying. She wanted him to pray with her, and he asked what he could pray for, but she didn't know and couldn't tell him. She was completely unable to name one thing that he could ask God for her soul. All she wanted was the form of a minister's prayers. I can understand this; deathbeds reveal many secrets. I can't forget what I have seen of sick and dying people. This also leads me to believe that few people pray.

I cannot see your heart. I do not know your private history in spiritual things. But from what I see in the Bible and in the world, I know I can't ask you a more necessary question than the one I am asking now—DO YOU PRAY?

Study Guide

Reading this chapter, you can sense Ryle's disappointment and longing for Christians to see what they are missing by neglecting prayer. It seems to be one of the most common aspects, along with reading the Bible, that is often forgotten or shoved aside in the rush of everyday life.

In these questions, try and be honest, even if you don't agree with what Ryle has written. An honest answer will allow for more discussion, learning, and in the end, growth. But also, be open. Listen to others' opinions, test, and see if they line up with Scripture.

1. Ryle admits he used to think all, or most, Christians prayed. What is your view?
2. There is a distinction made between prayers, such as those repeated in institutions or quickly said over meals as ritual, and real, sincere, honest prayers. What is the difference?

3. Take a closer look at Acts 9:11. Why is this so significant compared to Paul's former life as a professed, praying Pharisee?
4. Ryle makes some bold statements regarding prayer and sin. What do you understand by this?
5. Comment on Colossians 4:2 concerning this chapter.

5

PRAYER BRINGS ENCOURAGEMENT

God's Part in Prayer

God has everything necessary to make prayer easy if we will only give it a try. All things are ready on His side. Every objection we have, He has already anticipated. Every difficulty is provided for. The crooked places are made straight, and the rough places are made smooth. There is no excuse left for those of us who don't pray.

There is a way for every person, however sinful and unworthy they are, to draw near to God the Father. Jesus Christ has opened that way by the sacrifice He made for us on the cross. The holiness and justice of God shouldn't frighten sinners and keep them away. They just need to cry to God in the name of Jesus—plead the atoning blood of Jesus—and they will find God on a throne of grace, willing and ready to hear them. The name of Jesus is a passport for our prayers that never fails. In that name, we can come near to God with boldness, and ask with confidence; God is ready to hear us. Isn't this an encouragement?

There is an advocate and intercessor that is always waiting to present the prayers of those who will let Him do so—Jesus Christ. He mixes our prayers with the incense of His own almighty intercession so that they go up as a sweet fragrance before the throne of God. Poor as they are, they are mighty and powerful in the hand of our High Priest.

A cheque without a signature at the bottom is nothing but a worthless piece of paper. The stroke of a pen gives it all its value. The prayer of a poor child of Adam is weak on its own, but once endorsed by the hand of Jesus it can achieve a lot. There was an officer in the city of Rome who was appointed to always have his doors open to receive any Roman citizen who applied to him for help. It is the same with the ear of Jesus, who is always open to the cry of everyone who wants mercy and grace. It's His role to help us. Our prayer is His delight. When you look at this, isn't this an encouragement?

The Holy Spirit is always ready to help our weakness in prayer. It's one part of His role to assist us in our efforts to speak with God. We don't need to be depressed and worried with the fear of not knowing what to say, the Spirit will give us words if we just ask for His help. He will give us "thoughts that breathe and words that burn." The prayers of us as Christians are the inspiration of the Spirit —the work of the Holy Spirit who lives in us as the Spirit of grace and prayer. Surely we can hope to be heard. It's not us who are simply praying, but the Holy Spirit pleading in us. When we think about this, isn't this an encouragement?

His Promises

There are incredible and precious promises to those of us who pray. What did Jesus mean when He said these words?

- *"Ask, and it will be given to you; seek, and you will find; knock, and it will be opened to you. For everyone who asks receives, and the one who seeks finds, and to the one who knocks it will be opened"* (Matt. 7:7-8).
- *"And whatever you ask in prayer, you will receive, if you have faith"* (Matt 21:22).
- *"Whatever you ask in my name, this I will do, that the Father may be glorified in the Son. If you ask me anything in my name, I will do it"* (John 14:13-14).
- What did He mean when in the parables of the friend at midnight and the persistent widow? (Luke 11:5 and 18:1).

Think about these verses. If these are not an encouragement to pray, then the words have no meaning at all.

There are wonderful examples in the Bible of the power of prayer. Nothing seems to be too great, too hard, or too difficult for prayer to do. It has achieved things that seemed impossible and out of reach. It has won victories over fire, air, earth, and water. Prayer opened the Red Sea. Prayer brought water from the rock and bread from heaven. Prayer made the sun stand still. Prayer brought down fire from the sky on Elijah's sacrifice. Prayer turned the counsel of Ahithophel into foolishness. Prayer overthrew the army of Sennacherib.

No wonder Mary, Queen of Scots, said, "I fear John Knox's prayers more than an army of ten thousand men."

Prayer has healed the sick. Prayer has raised the dead. Prayer has brought about the conversion of souls. "The child of many prayers," a Christian once said to Augustine's mother, "shall never perish." Prayer, suffering, and faith can do anything. Nothing seems impossible when a man has the spirit of adoption. "*Let Me alone*" (Exodus 32:10), are the remarkable words of God to Moses, when Moses was about to intercede for the children of Israel. The Chaldee translation writes it as, "leave off praying." As long as Abraham asked mercy for Sodom, the Lord went on giving. He never stopped giving it until Abraham stopped praying. When you think about this, isn't this an encouragement?

What more can a person want to guide them to grow spiritually, than the things I have just told you about prayer? What more can be done to make the path to the mercy seat easier, and to remove all obstacles from the sinner's way? If the demons in hell had a door like this opened before them, they would jump for joy, and scream with happiness.

But where will the person that neglects such amazing encouragement hide their head? What can possibly be said for the person who dies without prayer after all of this? I hope that you are not that person.

So, I have to ask—DO YOU PRAY?

Study Guide

We all need encouragement in our lives, and often, we look to family, friends, books, television, and even church. But this chapter indicates that we don't have to look much further than prayer to find it. The promises and hope in Jesus that are linked with prayer should be encouraging enough. The power behind and in prayer is far greater than we realize, and Ryle is convinced that it should lift us up and motivate us.

1. "God has everything necessary to make prayer easy." This is a very interesting statement. What do you think about it?
2. Is your prayer life easier because of everything God has done or harder?
3. Read Romans 8:34. What do you understand about Jesus interceding for us?
4. "Prayer, suffering, and faith can do anything." What does this mean?
5. Do you find encouragement in your own prayers?
6. Read and comment on Philippians 4:6-7.

6

DILIGENT PRAYER IS THE SECRET TO HOLINESS

Two Different Types of Christian

Without question or argument, we can agree that there is a vast difference among true Christians. There is a huge gap between those on the frontline and those in the rearguard of God's army.

We are all fighting the same good fight, but some fight more courageously than others! We are all doing the Lord's work, but some do much more than others! We are all light in the Lord, but some shine brighter than others! We are all running the same race, but some go faster than others! We all love the same Lord and Savior, but some love Him more than others! My question for us Christians is whether this is true or not.

There are some Christians who never seem to be able to move on from the time of their conversion. They are born again, but they remain babies, all their lives. They are learners in Christ's school, but they never seem to get beyond ABC and the lowest grade. They get inside the sheep pen, but once there, they lie down and go no further. Year after year you see they have the same old sins, and hear from them the same old experience.

You notice they have the same spiritual appetite—squeamish about anything but the milk of the Word, and the dislike of strong meat. They have the same childishness, the same weakness, the same small thinking, the same small hearts, the same lack of interest in anything beyond their own little circle, which you noticed ten years ago. They are definitely pilgrims, but pilgrims like the Gideonites of the Bible—their bread is always dry and moldy, their shoes always old and clumsy, and their clothes always full of holes and torn. I say this with sadness and grief. But I ask any real Christian, isn't this true?

Then, there are others who always seem to be moving forwards. They grow like grass after rain. They increase like Israel in Egypt. They press on like Gideon, even though they are sometimes "*exhausted yet pursuing*" (Judges 8:4). They are always adding grace to grace, faith to faith, and strength to strength. Every time you meet them, their hearts seem larger, and their spiritual stature bigger, taller, and stronger. Every year they appear to see more, and know more, and believe more, and feel more in their faith.

They don't just have good works to prove the reality of their faith, but they are passionate about them. They don't just do well, but they are never tired of doing good. They attempt great things, and they do great things. When they fail, they try again, and when they fall they soon get up again. And all this time, they think they are poor, unprofitable servants, and feel as though they are doing nothing at all.

These are the ones that make Christianity lovely and beautiful for everyone to see. Even those outside the church praise them, and the selfish people of the world have good opinions of them. These are the ones that are always good to see, to be with, and to hear. When you meet them, you could believe that, like Moses, they had just come from the presence of God. When you leave them, you feel encouraged by their company, as if your heart had been near a fire. I know such people are rare. My question is, isn't it just like this?

What Is the Difference?

Now, how can we account for the difference I have just described? What is the reason that some believers are so much brighter and holier than others? I believe the difference in nineteen out of twenty cases comes from different habits in personal prayer. I believe that those who are not very holy, hardly pray, and those who are very holy, pray a lot.

I am sure this opinion will surprise some people. I have little doubt that many see great holiness as a special kind of gift, which only a few pretend to aim at. They admire it from a distance in books. They think it's beautiful when they see an example near them. But other than something that's within reach of only a very few, such a notion never seems to enter their minds. In short, they consider it a kind of monopoly granted to a few favored believers, but certainly not to everyone.

Now, I believe that this is a very dangerous mistake. I believe that spiritual, as well as natural, greatness depends far more on what is within everyone's reach than on anything else. Of course, I don't say we have a right to expect a miraculous handout of intellectual gifts. But I will say this, that when a person is born again, whether they are very holy or not, depends mainly on his own diligence in using God's appointed methods. And I can confidently add that the principal way that most believers have become great in the church, is through the habit of diligent and private prayer.

Look at the lives of the brightest and best of God's servants, whether they were in the Bible or not. See what is written about Moses, David, Daniel, and Paul. Notice what is recorded about Luther and Bradford, the Reformers. Observe what is told of the private devotions of Whitefield, Cecil, Venn, Bickersteth, and M'Cheyne. Tell me about any of these saints and martyrs that did not have this obvious, prominent sign—they were men of prayer. You can depend on this, prayer is power!

Prayer brings a fresh and continued outpouring of the Spirit. He alone begins the work of grace in a person's heart. He alone can carry it forward and make it prosper. But the Spirit loves to be begged, and those who ask the most will always receive the most of His influence.

Prayer is the most definite cure against the devil and nagging sins. Any sin that is properly prayed against will never stand strong. The devil will never hold dominion over us in any area that we ask the Lord to deal with. But, we must state our case to our heavenly Doctor, so He can give us daily relief. We must drag those demons that are pestering us to Jesus' feet, and cry to Him to send them back to hell.

Do you wish to grow in grace and be a very holy Christian? If that is what you wish, then it's clear that you could not have a more important question than this—DO YOU PRAY?

Study Guide

Holiness is the highest point in a Christian's walk. It is what God calls us to be, but it is not always as easy as we think. However, Ryle comments that a life of continual prayer is the secret door to attaining this. According to him, someone who prays will not lead a life of sin, and therefore be holy.

Make notes as you answer these questions. Keep a journal of your thoughts and answers. It is the best way to show progress in what the Holy Spirit is teaching and showing you. Keep your Bible open and refer to verses as often as possible—even do your own study of related scriptures.

1. According to this chapter, there are two types of Christian. Can you describe each one in your own words or find a verse that does this?
2. Which one best describes you right now?
3. What do you understand by the word 'holiness'?
4. What does prayer allow the Holy Spirit to do?
5. Ryle says that prayer is a cure against the devil and nagging sins. Do you agree?

6. Is it possible that prayer can be the path to holiness? How?

7

PRAYER AND BACKSLIDING

What Is Backsliding?

There is such a thing as going backward in your faith after starting well once you've been born again. You might run well for a season, like the Galatians, and then turn away to false teachers. You might loudly claim your belief, while your feelings are warm, as Peter did; and then, in the hour of trial, deny your Lord. You may lose your first love, as the Ephesians did. You might cool down in your passion to do good, like Mark, the companion of Paul. You might follow an apostle for a season, and then, like Demas, go back to the world. All these things you could do. It's a miserable thing to be a backslider. Of all the terrible things that can happen to a person, I think this is the worst.

A stranded ship, a broken-winged eagle, a garden covered in weeds, a harp without strings, a church in ruins—all these are sad sights, but a backslider is still a much sadder sight. I don't doubt that true grace can ever be extinguished or a true relationship with Jesus can ever be broken off. But I do believe that a person might fall away so far that they can lose sight of their own grace, and question their own salvation. And if this is not hell, it's certainly very close to it. A wounded conscience, a mind sick of itself, a memory full of self-criticism, a heart pierced through with the Lord's arrows, a spirit broken with a burden of accusation—this is all a taste of hell. It's hell on earth. The wise saying of Solomon is serious and worth noting, *"The backslider in heart will be filled with the fruit of his ways"* (Prov 14:14).

Why Christians Backslide

Now, what is the cause of most backsliding? I believe that one of the main causes is neglecting private prayer. Of course, the secret history of every person's fall from grace will not be known until the last day. I can only give my opinion as a minister of Christ, and a student of the heart. That opinion is, I repeat it clearly, that backsliding generally first begins with neglect of personal prayer.

Bibles read without prayer, sermons heard without prayer, marriages contracted without prayer, homes chosen without prayer, friendships formed without prayer, the daily act of private prayer itself rushed, or performed without heart— these are the downward steps that many Christians descend to a condition of spiritual paralysis, or they reach the point where God allows them to experience a significant fall.

This is the process that produces the lingering Lots, the unstable Samsons, the wife-idolizing Solomons, the inconsistent Asas, the pliable Jehosaphats, the over-careful Martha's —and there are so many of them to be found in the church. Often, the simple history of such cases is this: They became careless about private prayer.

You can be very sure that people fall in private, long before they fall in public. They are backsliders on their knees long before they backslide openly to the eyes of the world. Like Peter, they first ignore Jesus' warning to watch and pray; and then, like Peter, their strength is gone, and in the hour of temptation, they deny Him.

The world takes notice of their fall, and loudly mocks them, but doesn't know the real reason. Origen, the theologian and Father of the Faith in the early centuries after Jesus' death, ended up offering incense to an idol after being threatened by heathens with a punishment worse than death. Those non-believers boasted and gloated at his cowardice and denial of God, but they did not know the facts. Origen tells us in his writings, that on that very morning he had left his room in a rush and did not finish his usual time of prayer.

If you really are a true Christian, I trust you will never be a backslider. But if you don't wish to be a backsliding Christian, remember the question I ask you—DO YOU PRAY?

Study Guide

Backsliding is very common and often happens when we least expect it. It's why we constantly need the Lord in our lives and have to keep the relationship secure. Prayer maintains our communion and access to God open. True prayer will always keep you honest before God.

Don't be embarrassed to share moments when you have felt far or drifted from God. Be open about your answers. It exposes our need for Jesus and His redeeming work in our lives. Again, write down your answers or thoughts so that you can refer back to them.

1. Ryle opens up with 5 biblical examples of backsliders. Which one do you identify most within your own life?
2. What do you understand by the verse, Proverbs 14:14?
3. According to the author, what is one of the main causes of backsliding?
4. Do you agree with the statement that backsliders fall in private long before they do in public?
5. Look at Hebrews 10:39 in this context. What do you understand about this verse?

8

PRAYER AND CONTENTMENT

We live in a world where there is so much sorrow; it has always been this way since sin came in. There cannot be sin without sorrow, and until sin is driven out of the world, it is useless for anyone to think they can escape sorrow.

Some people have a larger cup of sorrow to drink than others. But there are very few who live long without sorrows or worry of some kind. Our bodies, property, families, children, relatives, servants, friends, neighbors, or jobs—every one of these is a fountain of worry. Sicknesses, deaths, losses, disappointments, partings, separations, ingratitude, slander—all these are common things. We can't get through life without them; they will find us sooner or later. The greater our attachment to things and people are, the deeper our troubles will be; and the more we love, the more we will have to cry about.

Prayer Is the Answer

And what is the best recipe for happiness in a world like this? How can we get through this valley of tears with the least amount of pain? I don't know of any better recipe than the habit of taking everything to God in prayer.

This is the simple advice that the Bible gives, both in the Old and in the New Testament. What does the Psalmist say?

- *"Call upon me in the day of trouble; I will deliver you, and you shall glorify me"* (Psalm 50:15).
- *"Cast your burden on the Lord, and he will sustain you; he will never permit the righteous to be moved"* (Psalm 55:22).

What does Paul say?

- *"Do not be anxious about anything, but in everything by prayer and supplication with thanksgiving let your requests be made known to God. And the peace of God, which surpasses all understanding, will guard your hearts and your minds in Christ Jesus"* (Phil 4:6-7).

What does James say?

- *"Is anyone among you suffering? Let him pray"* (James 5:13).

This was the habit and custom of all the believers whose history is recorded in the Bible. This is what Jacob did when he feared his brother Esau. This is what Moses did when the people were ready to stone him in the wilderness. This is what Joshua did when Israel was defeated before Ai. This is what David did when he was in danger at Keilah. This is what Hezekiah did when he received the letter from Sennacherib. This is what the church did when Peter was put in prison. This is what Paul did when he was thrown into jail at Philippi.

Jesus Will Take Our Sorrows

The only way to really be happy in a world like this is to always be casting all our cares on God. Trying to carry our own burdens is what often makes us as Christians sad. If we only tell our troubles to God, He will help us to bear them as easily as Samson picked up and carried the gates of Gaza. If we decide to keep them to ourselves, then one day we will find that even a grasshopper is a burden.

There is a friend that is always waiting to help us if we will only offload our sorrow onto Him; a friend who had compassion for the poor, sick, and sorrowful, when He was on the earth; a friend who knows the heart of man, because He lived thirty-three years as a man amongst us; a friend who can cry with those who mourn, because He was a man of sorrows and knew grief very well; a friend who can help us, for there was no human pain that He could not cure. That friend is Jesus Christ.

The way to be happy is to always open our hearts to Him. Oh, that we were all like that poor Christian slave, when he was threatened and punished, he just answered, "I must tell the Lord."

Jesus can make all those who trust Him and call on Him happy, whatever their circumstances may be. He can give them peace of heart in a prison, contentment in the midst of poverty, comfort in times of grief, and joy when death is near. There is a mighty fullness in Him for all those who believe in Him—a fullness that is ready to be poured out on every one that asks in prayer. If only people could understand that happiness does not depend on physical circumstances but the state of the heart.

Prayer can make our cross lighter, no matter how heavy it is—it can bring One who will help us to bear them. Prayer can open a door for us when our way seems closed off—it can bring One who will say, "*This is the way, walk in it*" (Isaiah 30:12). Prayer can let in a ray of hope when all our earthly prospects seem dark—it can bring One who will say, "*I will never leave you nor forsake you*" (Heb 13:5). Prayer can give relief to us when those we love most have died, and the world feels empty—it can bring One who can fill the gap in Our hearts with Himself, and say to the waves within, "*Peace! Be still!*" (Mark 4:39). If only people were not so much like Hagar in the wilderness, blind to the well of living waters that are so near to them! (Genesis 21:19).

I want you to be happy, and I know I cannot ask you a more useful question than this—DO YOU PRAY?

Study Guide

We all long to be content—with each other, with our lives, with ourselves. But the truth is we often aren't. Jesus can bring us joy, peace, and contentment even in the worst circumstances if we only pray.

Discussing your thoughts and answers with others will not only challenge you to come to grips with the topics being discussed but also provide enlightenment when you might least expect it. If you are in a group, allow time for these moments of discussion. If not, make time to talk them over with a pastor or someone you trust.

1. Do you agree with the equation set out here, that sin equals sorrow?
2. Ryle mentions a recipe for happiness in this world. What is it? Do you agree?
3. What, according to the author, "often makes us as Christians sad"?
4. Read 1 Timothy 6:6-7. How does contentment add to our lives as Christians?
5. Do you think it's possible to be a discontent Christian?
6. Is the peace that passes understanding the same as contentment, or not?

9

TO THOSE WHO DON'T PRAY

Let me say one last thing to those who do not pray. I don't think that everyone who reads this book will be people who pray. If you are a prayerless person, let me speak to you now on God's behalf.

I can only warn you, but I do so seriously. I warn you that you are in a very dangerous position! If you die in your present state, you are a lost soul, and you will only rise again to be eternally miserable. I warn you, that of all professing Christians, you have no excuse. There is no good reason that you can show for living without prayer.

No Excuse for Not Praying

It is useless to say you don't know how to pray. Prayer is the simplest act in religion: it's simply speaking to God. It doesn't need learning, wisdom, or book-knowledge to begin it. It needs nothing but heart and will. The weakest baby can cry when he is hungry. The poorest beggar can hold out his hand for coins and doesn't wait to find eloquent words. The most ignorant man will find something to say to God if he only thinks about it.

It is useless to say you don't have a convenient place to pray in; any man can find a place private enough if he is desperate enough. Jesus prayed on a mountain, Peter on the house-top, Isaac in the field, Nathanael under the fig tree, Jonah in the whale's belly. Any place may become a closet, a room, and a Bethel, and be to us the presence of God.

It is useless to say you have no time. There is plenty of time if people will only use it properly. Time may be short, but time is always long enough for prayer. Daniel had all the affairs of a kingdom to deal with, and yet he prayed three times a day. David was ruler over a mighty nation, and yet he says, *"Evening and morning and at noon I utter my complaint and moan, and he hears my voice"* (Psalm 55:17). When time is really important, time can always be found.

It is useless to say you cannot pray until you have faith and a new heart, and that you must sit still and wait for them. This is to add sin to sin. It is bad enough to be unconverted and going to hell, it's even worse to say, "I know it, but I won't cry for mercy." This is an argument that has no standing in the Bible.

- *"Seek the Lord while he may be found;"* Isaiah said, *"call upon him while he is near"* (Isaiah 55:6).

- "*Take with you words and return to the Lord,*" says Hosea (Hosea 14:2).
- "*Repent, therefore, of this wickedness of yours, and pray to the Lord,*" says Peter to Simon Magus (Acts 8:22).

If you want faith and a new heart, go and cry to the Lord for them. The very attempt to pray has often been the revival of a dead soul. There is no devil so dangerous as a dumb devil.

A Warning

What kind of a person are you not to ask anything of God? Have you made a covenant with death and hell? Are you at peace with the worm and the fire? Have you got no sins that need to be forgiven? Have you got no fear of eternal torment? Have you got no desire for heaven? Wake up from your foolishness! Think about where you will end up! Rise up and call on God! A day is coming when many will pray loudly, "Lord, Lord, open up for us," but it will all be too late. Many people will cry to the rocks to fall on them, and the hills to cover them; those who would never cry to God.

In love, I warn you. Watch out, this could be the end of your soul. Salvation is very near to you. Don't lose heaven because you never asked.

Study Guide

Ryle's tone may be direct and a little harsh, but it shows his evangelical passion to warn and save those who are drifting or lost. If this chapter finds you squirming at the words or trying to avoid the finger that is pointing out of the pages, don't run. As he says, 'In love, I warn you.' The Lord is merciful and His grace is there for all of us in whatever stage or state we are in.

Work through these questions with a softness in your heart.

1. Why do people not pray? What stops them?
2. What is your answer to the excuses listed in this chapter:
3. I don't know how to pray
4. I don't have a place to pray
5. I don't have time to pray
6. I have no faith to pray
7. Look at 1 Samuel 12:23. What do you understand about this?
8. The disciples needed help with prayer. They asked Jesus (Luke 11:1). Do you need help with praying? Ask.

10

TO THOSE WHO WANT SALVATION

Let me speak to those who really want salvation but don't know what steps to take or where to begin. I hope that there are some like that who read this, and so I must offer you encouragement and advice.

Taking the First Step

In every journey, there must be a first step. There must be a change from sitting still to moving forward. The travels of Israel from Egypt to Canaan were long and tiring. Forty years passed before they crossed Jordan, yet there was someone who first moved when they marched from Ramah to Succoth. When does a person really take their first step in coming out from sin and the world? They do it on the day when they first pray with their heart.

In every building, the first stone must be laid, and the first blow must be struck. The ark took 120 years to build, but there was a day when Noah had to take his ax and start cutting the first tree down to form it. The temple of Solomon was a glorious building, but there was a day when the first huge stone was laid at the foot of Mount Moriah. When does the building of the Spirit really begin to appear in a person's heart? It begins when they first pour out their heart to God in prayer.

If you want salvation, and you want to know what to do, I advise you to go right now to Jesus Christ in the first private place you can find and beg Him in prayer to save your soul.

Tell Him that you've heard that He receives sinners and has said, *"Whoever comes to me I will never cast out"* (John 6:37). Tell Him that you are a poor and terrible sinner and that you come to Him on the faith of His own invitation. Tell Him you put yourself completely into His hands—that you feel evil and helpless, and hopeless in yourself—and that unless He saves you, you have no hope at all to be saved. Beg Him to deliver you from the guilt, power, and consequences of sin. Beg Him to forgive you and wash you in His own blood. Beg Him to give you a new heart and to put the Holy Spirit in your soul. Beg Him to give you grace, faith, will, and power to be His disciple and servant from this day forever. Go right now, and tell these things to Jesus if you really are sincere and true about your soul.

Tell Him in your own way, and your own words. If a doctor came to see you when you're sick, you could tell him where you felt pain. If your heart feels the disease in it, surely you can find something to tell Christ.

Don't Doubt

Don't doubt His willingness to save you, because you are a sinner. It's Jesus' occupation to save sinners. He says, "*I have not come to call the righteous but sinners to repentance*" (Luke 5:32).

Don't wait because you feel unworthy. Don't wait for anything of anybody—waiting comes from the devil. Just as you are, go to Jesus. The worse you are, the more you need Him. You will never fix yourself by staying away.

Don't be afraid because your prayer is stuttering, your words weak, and your language is poor. Jesus can understand you. Just as a mother understands the first babblings of her baby, so the Savior understands sinners. He can read a sigh, and see a meaning in a groan.

Don't be discouraged because you don't get an answer immediately. While you are speaking, Jesus is listening. If He delays an answer, it is only for wise reasons, and to see if you are sincere. Pray on, and the answer will come. Even though it takes a while, wait for it. It will surely come at last.

If you have any desire to be saved, remember the advice I have given you today. Act on it honestly and completely, and you will be saved.

Study Guide

Salvation is the greatest mystery and gift that Jesus gave to us through His death on the cross. By defeating sin, He opened a way for us to have fellowship with God, so we may speak to Him and have access to all He has for us. Ryle was known to have a heart for those who were not yet saved, and it shows as he takes the time to speak on this.

If you are not yet saved or are wanting the life, peace, and joy that Jesus offers, don't wait. Open your mouth and ask Him for it. Confess your sin and where you have come from. He will listen and respond!

1. What are the 4 things that Ryle lists that hold us back from coming to Jesus?
2. Look at John 6:37. What does the word 'never' tell you?
3. Look at 1 John 1:9. It is a powerful verse about how Jesus will respond when we come to Him.
4. If you are not yet saved, tell someone. Ask them to help you if you need it.
5. If you are already saved, share with someone how Jesus found you and rescued you.

11

TO THOSE WHO PRAY

Let me speak to those who do pray. I trust that some who read this book know what prayer is, and have the Spirit of adoption. To all of you, I have a few words of brotherly advice and encouragement. The incense offered in the tabernacle was ordered to be made in a particular way. Not every kind of incense would do. Let us remember this, and be careful about what we pray about and how we pray.

To those who pray, if I know anything of a Christian's heart, you are often sick of your own prayers. You know the meaning of the Apostle's words, "*When I want to do right, evil lies close at hand*" (Rom. 7:21), as you go down on your knees. You can understand David's words, "*I hate the double-minded*" (Psalm 119:113). You can sympathize with that poor converted person, who was once heard praying, "Lord, deliver me from all my enemies, and, above all, from that bad man myself!" There are few Christians who don't often find prayer to be a season of conflict.

The devil hates seeing us on our knees, yet I believe we should be suspicious of any prayers which cost us nothing. I believe we are very poor judges of the goodness of our prayers, and that the prayer which pleases us the least, often pleases God the most. Listen then, as a colleague in the Christian warfare, to offer you a few words of encouragement. At least we all feel that we must pray. We cannot give it up. We must go on.

Reverence and Humility in Prayer

I want to draw your attention to the importance of reverence and humility in prayer. Let us never forget what we are, and what a solemn thing it is to speak with God. Let us beware of rushing into His presence with carelessness and irreverence. Let us say to ourselves, "I am on holy ground, this is the gate of heaven. If I don't mean what I say, I am messing with God. If I love sin in my heart, the Lord will not hear me." Let us keep in mind the words of Solomon, *"Be not rash with your mouth, nor let your heart be hasty to utter a word before God, for God is in heaven and you are on earth"* (Eccles. 5:2). When Abraham spoke to God, he said, *"I who am but dust and ashes"* (Gen 18:27). When Job spoke, he said, *"Behold, I am of small account"* (Job 40:4). Let us do the same.

Praying Spiritually

Next, I want to highlight the importance of praying spiritually. What I mean by this, is that we should always have the help of the Spirit in our prayers, and be careful of formality. Everything spiritual can easily become a method, and this is especially true of private prayer. We may get into the habit of using the best possible words, making the most in scriptural requests, and yet do it all by repetition without feeling it, and walk around an old beaten path every day, like a horse tied to a mill.

I want to touch on this point with caution and care. I know that daily there are great things we need and that there is nothing necessarily formal in asking for these things by using the same words. The world, the devil, and our hearts are the same every day, and out of necessity, we have to do the same old things every day. But we must be very careful on this point. If the skeleton and outline of our prayers become an order of doing things out of habit, then let us make sure that the clothing and filling up of our prayer is as of the Spirit as much as possible.

When it comes to praying out of a book, it is a habit I don't encourage. If we can tell our doctors the state of our bodies without a book, we should be able to tell the state of our hearts to God. I have no objection to a man using crutches when he is recovering from a broken leg; it's better to use crutches than not to walk at all. But if I saw him on crutches for the rest of his life, I wouldn't congratulate him. I would rather see him become strong enough to throw his crutches away.

Regular Prayer

Next, I want to talk about the importance of making prayer a regular part of life, and the value of making regular times in the day for prayer. God is a God of order. The hours for morning and evening sacrifice in the Jewish temple were not there for no reason. Disorder is one of the fruits of sin, but I don't want to condemn anyone.

I only say that it is essential to your heart's health to make praying a part of every 24 hours in your life. Just as you give time to eating, sleeping, and business, so also give time to prayer. Choose your own hours and seasons. If nothing else, speak with God in the morning, before you speak with the world; and speak with God at night after you are finished with the world. But establish in your minds that prayer is one of the most important duties of every day. Don't push it into a corner. Don't give it the scraps and leftovers of your day. Whatever else you make a duty of, make a duty of prayer.

Perseverance in Prayer

Next, I want to look at the importance of perseverance in prayer. Once you have begun the habit, never give it up. Your heart will sometimes say, "You have had family prayers; what's the harm of skipping private prayer?" Your body will sometimes say, "You are not well, or sleepy, or tired; you don't need to pray." Your mind will sometimes say, "You have important business to attend to; cut your prayers short." Look at these suggestions as coming directly from the devil. They are as good as saying, "Neglect your soul."

I don't mean that your prayers always have to be the same length, but don't let any excuse make you give up prayer. Paul didn't say, "*Continue steadfastly in prayer*," and "*Pray without ceasing*" for nothing (Col 4:2, 1 Thess 5:17). He didn't mean people should always be on their knees, like the Euchitæ sect used to think. But he did mean that our prayers should be like the continual burnt offering—a thing constantly persevered in every day—that it should be like seed-time and harvest, and summer and winter—a thing that should always happen at regular seasons—that it should be like the fire on the altar, not always consuming sacrifices, but never completely going out.

Never forget that you can link your morning and evening devotions with an endless chain of short prayers said throughout the day. Even in company, or business, or in the streets, you can be silently sending up little winged messengers to God, as Nehemiah did in the presence of King Artaxerxes. (Neh 2:4). And don't think that the time given to God is wasted. A nation does not become poorer because it loses a day each week of the year by keeping the Sabbath. A Christian is never a loser in the long run by persevering in prayer.

Sincerity in Prayer

Another point is the importance of sincerity in prayer. It's not necessary for someone to have to shout, scream, or be very loud to prove that they are sincere. But we should be passionate, sincere, enthusiastic, and ask as if we were really interested in what we were doing. It is the "*effective fervent prayer*" that "*avails much*," and not the cold, sleepy, lazy, lifeless one (James 5:16 NKJV). This is the lesson taught to us by the expressions used in the Bible about prayer. It's called "crying," "knocking," "wrestling," "laboring," and "striving."

This is the lesson taught to us by biblical examples.

- Jacob said to the angel at Penuel, "*I will not let You go unless You bless me!*" (Gen 32:26).
- Daniel pleaded with God, "*O Lord, hear! O Lord, forgive! O Lord, listen and act! Do not delay for Your own sake, my God*" (Daniel 9:19).
- It was written about Jesus, "*In the days of His flesh, when He had offered up prayers and supplications, with vehement cries and tears*" (Heb 5:7).

How different these are to many of our own prayers that seem tame and lukewarm in comparison! I am sure God would say to many of us, "You do not really want what you pray for!" Let us try to fix this fault. Let us knock loudly at the door of grace, like the character Mercy in the book, Pilgrim's Progress, as though we will die unless we are heard. Let us get it into our heads that cold prayers are a sacrifice without fire. Let us remember the story of Demosthenes, the great orator when a man came and wanted him to plead his case. He listened to the man as he told his story without paying attention. When the man saw this, he cried out that what he was saying was all true and worthy to be heard. "Ah!" said Demosthenes, "I believe you now."

Praying with Faith

Next, we talk about the importance of praying with faith. We should try our best to believe that our prayers are always heard and that if we ask things according to God's will, they will always be answered. This is the simple command of Jesus: *"Therefore I say to you, whatever things you ask when you pray, believe that you receive them, and you will have them"* (Mark 11:24). Faith is to prayer what the feather is to the arrow: without it, prayer will not hit the mark. We should grow in the habit of pleading promises in our prayers. We should take His promise, and say, *"Now, O Lord God, the word which You have spoken concerning Your servant and concerning his house, establish it forever and do as You have said"* (2 Sam 7:25). This was the habit of Jacob, Moses, and David. Psalm 119 is full of things asked, *"according to Your word."*

Above all, we should grow in the habit of expecting answers to our prayers. We should be like the merchant, who sends his ships to sea, and not be satisfied unless we see some return. Unfortunately, more than any other points, Christians fall short on this. The church at Jerusalem prayed without ceasing for Peter in prison; but when the prayer was answered, they could hardly believe it. (Acts 12:15.) It is a serious saying of Robert Traill's, "There is no surer mark of trifling in prayer, than when men are careless what they get by prayer."

Boldness in Prayer

Furthermore, I want to emphasize the importance of boldness in prayer. There is a familiarity in some people's prayers, which I don't like. But there is such a thing as a holy boldness, which should be desired.

- I am talking about the boldness like that of Moses when he pleaded with God not to destroy Israel; *"Why should the Egyptians speak, and say, 'He brought them out to harm them, to kill them in the mountains, and to consume them from the face of the earth'? Turn from Your fierce wrath, and relent from this harm to Your people"* (Exod 32:12).
- I am talking about the boldness like that of Joshua when the children of Israel were defeated before Ai: *"Then what will You do for Your great name?"* (Joshua 7:9).
- It's the same boldness for which Luther was remarkable. Someone heard him praying and said, "What a spirit, what a confidence was in his very expressions! With such a reverence he sued, as one begging of God, and yet with such hope and assurance, as if he spoke with a loving father or friend."
- This is the boldness that distinguished Bruce, a great Scot of the 17th century. His prayers were said to be "like bolts shot up into heaven."

Sadly, we also fall short in this area. We do not properly realize the privileges we have as believers. We do not plead as often as we should, "Lord, are we not Your people? Is it not for Your glory that we should be sanctified? Is it not for Your honor that the Gospel should increase?"

Fullness in Prayer

Next, I want to look at the importance of fullness in prayer. Jesus warns us against the Pharisees who made long prayers for show; and commands us not to use vain repetitions when we pray. But, on the other hand, He approves of large and long devotions, because He also continued all night in prayer to God. We probably won't ever be guilty of praying too much, but rather that Christians these days pray too little. On average, isn't the actual amount of time that many Christians give to prayer very small? These questions can't be answered satisfactorily, but I am afraid that most people's private devotions are very short and limited—just enough to prove they are alive, and no more. We seem to want and need very little from God. We have little to confess, little to ask for, and little to thank Him for. This is wrong.

There is nothing more common than hearing believers complaining that they don't get along with each other. They tell us that they don't grow in grace, even though they want it. Isn't it actually true that many have as much grace as they ask for? Isn't it true that they have little because they ask little? The cause of their weakness is in their own stunted, clipped, contracted, hurried, little, narrow, small prayers. They have not, because they ask not.

We are not poor in Christ but ourselves. Jesus says, "*Open your mouth wide, and I will fill it*" (Psalm 81:10). But we are like the king of Israel, who struck the ground three times and stopped when he was supposed to have struck it five or six times (2 Kings 13:18).

Specific Prayer

Next is the importance of being specific in prayer. We should not be content with general requests. We should specify our wants and needs before the throne of grace. It shouldn't be enough to confess we are sinners, we should name the sins that our conscience tells us we are guilty of. It shouldn't be enough to ask for holiness, we should name the characteristics that we feel we are lacking the most. It shouldn't be enough to tell the Lord we are in trouble, we should describe our trouble and all its details.

- That is what Jacob did when he feared his brother Esau. He tells God exactly what it is that he fears. (Gen 32:11)
- That is what Eliezer did when he looked for a wife for his master's son. He precisely names what he wants before God (Gen 24:12)
- This is what Paul did when he had a thorn in the flesh. He asked the Lord about this. (2 Cor 12:8)
This is true faith and confidence.

We should believe that nothing is too small to be named before God. What would we think of the patient who told his doctor he was ill, but never went into details? What would we think of the wife who told her husband she was unhappy but did not specify the cause? What would we think of the child who told his father he was in trouble, but nothing more? Jesus is the true bridegroom of the soul—the true physician of the heart—the real father of all His people. Let us show that we feel this, by not holding anything back in our communications with Him. Let us hide no secrets from Him. Let us tell Him everything in our hearts.

Intercession in Prayer

Another point to look at is the importance of intercession in our prayers. We are all selfish by nature, and our selfishness is very apt to stick to us, even when we are born again. We tend to think only of our own souls—our own spiritual conflict—our own progress and to forget others. We all have to watch and make every effort against this tendency, especially in our prayers.

We should learn to become more aware of others in spirit and should stir ourselves up to list other names instead of just our own before the throne of grace. We should try to bear the whole world in our hearts—the lost, the Jews, the Roman Catholics, the body of true believers, the churches, the country in which we live, the congregation to which we belong, the household in which we live, the friends and relations we are connected with. We should plead for each one and all of these.

This is the highest act of compassion and kindness to others. He loves me best who loves me in his prayers. This is for our soul's health; it enlarges our sympathies and expands our hearts. This is for the benefit of the church. The wheels and cogs of the machinery that spreads the Gospel are oiled by prayer. We do as much for the Lord's cause when we intercede like Moses on the mountain, and when we fight like Joshua in the thick of the battle. This is to be like Jesus. He has the names of His people on His breast and shoulders as their high priest before the Father. What a privilege to be like Jesus! This is to be a true helper to ministers and pastors. If I must choose a congregation, give me one filled with people that pray.

Gratitude in Prayer

Then we need to talk about the importance of gratitude in prayer. I know that asking God is one thing, and praising God is another, but in the Bible, I see such a close connection between prayer and praise, that I cannot call a prayer true unless it has gratitude as part of it. Paul didn't say the following for nothing: *"But in everything by prayer and supplication, with thanksgiving, let your requests be made known to God"* (Phil 4:6). *"Continue earnestly in prayer, being vigilant in it with thanksgiving"* (Col 4:2).

It is because of God's mercy that we are not in hell. It is because of mercy that we have a hope in heaven. It is because of mercy that we live in a land of spiritual light. It is because of mercy that we have been called by the Spirit, and not left to reap the fruit of our own ways. It is because of mercy that we still live and have opportunities of glorifying God actively or passively. These kinds of thoughts should crowd our minds whenever we speak with God. We should never open our mouths in prayer without blessing God for that free grace by which we live, and for that loving-kindness that endures forever.

There has never been a prominent saint or Christian who was not full of thanksgiving. Paul hardly ever writes an epistle without beginning with gratitude. Men like Whitefield and Bickersteth were always overflowing with thanksgiving. If we want to be bright and shining lights in our day, we must have a spirit of praise, and above all, let our prayers be thankful prayers.

Being Alert in Prayer

Lastly, I mention the importance of being alert in your prayers. Prayer is that point at which you must be on your guard. It is here that true religion begins —here it flourishes, and here it decays. Tell me what a man's prayers are, and I will be able to tell you the state of his heart. Prayer is the spiritual pulse; by this, spiritual health can always be tested. Prayer is the spiritual barometer; by this, we can always know if it is clear or cloudy in our hearts. Let us keep a close, continual eye on our private devotions.

Here is the core, marrow, and backbone of our practical Christianity. Sermons, books, tracts, committee meetings, and fellowship with good people, are all good in their way, but they will never make up for the neglect of private prayer. Take a good look at the places, society, and companions that cause your hearts to drift away from communion with God, and make your prayers slow and ineffective. Be on your guard in those times. Observe the friends and duties that keep your heart in the right spiritual attitude, and when you are ready to speak with God—hold onto these and stay close. If you take care of your prayers, I can assure you that nothing will go very wrong with your heart.

I offer these points for your consideration and do so in all humility. I know no one who needs to be reminded of them more than I do myself, but I believe they are God's own truth, and I would like myself and everyone that I love to hold onto them even more.

I want the times we live in to be praying times. I want the Christians of our day to be praying Christians. I want the church of our age to be a praying church. My heart's desire and prayer in writing this is to promote a spirit of prayer. I want those who have never prayed yet, to rise up and call on God, and I want those who do pray, to make sure that they are not praying incorrectly.

Study Guide

This last chapter is almost a complete guidebook on prayer all by itself. Ryle goes through 12 different aspects at lightning speed, where others have taken pages to do so. Yet, he still manages to be clear, concise, and instructive.

1. Before listing his points, the author admits that often we are up one day and down the next. Is your prayer life like this? Why?
2. Look at the 12 aspects. Which one are you good at in your prayers? Which one are you really bad at getting right?

3. List them in your own order. Put those you are good at near the top, down to the ones you struggle with at the bottom.
4. How can you improve, grow, and mature in these areas?
5. After reading this book, has your view on prayer changed? Have you needed to change anything?

NOTES

ABOUT J. C. RYLE

John Charles Ryle was born in England on 10 May 1816. Growing up in an upper-class family, he had incredible access to education and sports and excelled in both. His skills in cricket and rowing earned him great fame during his school years, but just before writing his Final Exams, it all came crashing down.

A serious chest infection made him look at his Bible that he had neglected for so many years, and arriving at a church service late, was struck by the reading of Ephesians chapter 2. On hearing those words, he was born again in 1837.

Further studies and ambitions of entering politics came to an end with the double blow of his recurring infection and the demise of his father's bank. Instead, he trained in the Church of England becoming an ordained minister in 1841.

He had a few posts in local parishes, married, lost his wife, remarried before she too passed away until he finally moved to Suffolk in 1861 as vicar of All Saints. It was here that he became known for his direct approach to preaching and firm stand on the church's role and relevance as an evangelical light to the world. He wrote and published several books covering many different topics, including prayer, the church, and books of the Bible such as the Gospel of John.

In 1880, Ryle was appointed as the first Anglican Bishop of Liverpool under Prime Minister Benjamin Disraeli's advice. It was a position he used to build churches and mission halls to reach out to the urban areas that were growing around the city, which was always close to his evangelical mission.

At the age of 83, after losing his third wife, he retired and later died that same year in 1900.

BIBLIOGRAPHY

Crossway. (2001). *English Standard Version Bible*. Crossway Bibles.

Holman Bible Publishers. (2016). *The Holy Bible: NKJV New King James Version*. Holman Bible Publishers.

NOTES

NOTES

NOTES

www.ingramcontent.com/pod-product-compliance
Lightning Source LLC
LaVergne TN
LVHW010606070526
838199LV00063BA/5089